# The Sacred Sisterhood of
# Wonderful Wacky Women
## Book Two

# The Sacred Sisterhood of Wonderful Wacky Women
## Book Two

# by Suzy Toronto

Toronto Publishing, Inc.
Tangerine, Florida

For Launi…whose upside-down, inside-out, roller-coaster life is a constant reassurance that maybe…just maybe…I am normal after all. Together, as we navigate the inevitable detours of our lives, we remind each other that the journey *is* the destination. Without her, my life would be unbearable. God must surely love me to have sent such a friend.

# Table of Contents

Forward ........................................................... 7

They Who are More Than Friends ............................ 10

She Who Makes a Difference ..................................... 18

She Who is a Military Wife ....................................... 28

She Who is a Survivor .............................................. 36

She Who Does Foolish Things .................................... 44

She Who Never Gives Up ......................................... 52

She Who Loves to Travel ......................................... 62

She Who Loves to Shop ........................................... 70

She Who Reaches Out of Her Comfort Zone ............ 78

She Who Loves Shoes .............................................. 86

She Who *is* Christmas ............................................. 96

# Acknowledgments

To my business manager, Chantelle Joy, whom I affectionately call "the Rotweiller." She continually runs interference for me and watches my back. Her brutal honesty, unquestionable integrity and unconditional loyalty are blessings beyond measure – both personally and professionally. Without her, there would be no Suzy Toronto Studios.

To my licensing consultant, Joanne Fink, who, as she humbly puts it, "taught me how to fish." Somewhere along the way, through all the work, deadlines, edits and portfolios, we became more than business associates. We became close friends, and it has made a huge difference in my life.

To my graphic artist, Rob Thimm, whose creativity, imagination and graphic skills not only added a much-needed dimension to Suzy Toronto Studios, but gave me back my life.

To my parents, John and "Coke" Cyrocki, for always being such great cheerleaders. They always told me I could do anything I set my mind to. It has taken 50 years, but I finally believe them.

To my husband, Al, for catching the vision of what my work could be and then taking it there…for setting aside all he could have done, and, instead, spending his time hauling my art around the country, promoting my lines and building Suzy Toronto Studios…then never taking any of the credit. I'd do it all again, if I could do it all with him.

**Suzy Toronto**

# Forward

I've always believed that anyone who says she doesn't need a girlfriend, just hasn't found a good one yet. Now that I'm in my fifties, I believe it more than ever. I am such an over-the-top, girlfriend, girly-kind-of-girl that I can't imagine not having lots of women in my life. Over the years, I have been blessed to be surrounded by so many wonderful women who touched me, taught me and shaped me into the woman I am today. As I watched these friends go through both tragedies and triumphs in their lives, they taught me by their strength, drive, humor, love and compassion. I wanted to honor them, so I did it the only way I knew how. I drew and painted them as wild-haired, faceless characters and wrote short, poem-like stories to go with each as gifts of thanks, encouragement and congratulations. Before I knew it, the *Sacred Sisterhood of Wonderful Wacky Women* was born. It has since taken on a life of its own.

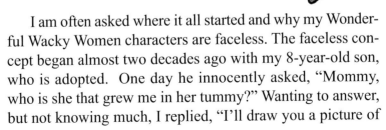

I am often asked where it all started and why my Wonderful Wacky Women characters are faceless. The faceless concept began almost two decades ago with my 8-year-old son, who is adopted. One day he innocently asked, "Mommy, who is she that grew me in her tummy?" Wanting to answer, but not knowing much, I replied, "I'll draw you a picture of her." I sketched out "She Who is With Child" and patterned it after myself that day, right down to my untamed hair and bare feet. I wanted him to think he was no better off and no worse off – he was just with the mom God wanted him to have. I left the character faceless to allow him to imagine what she looked like. It satisfied him, and he went on with his child's play.

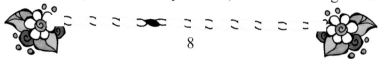

Even though the collection has close to 300 characters today, I like to think about the real woman who inspired that very first little drawing – a woman I have still never met – the biological mother of my son. She changed my life more than any other woman in my life. To her, I owe a great debt.

Like that very first character I drew so long ago, I continue to acknowledge ordinary women who have done extraordinary things. They have inspired, uplifted and empowered not only me, but all the women whose lives they've touched. They have made my life so full and rich that I am compelled to share their stories with you.

My favorite part of creating the art and prose for these women is the response I get from them when they find out they are in my book. Without exception, they are amazed and humbled that they have done anything noteworthy. Each claims to be just an ordinary woman, and until I brought it to their attention, didn't realize the extraordinary things they had accomplished. But the fact is, each of them touched another soul – and to do that is to walk on hallowed ground. Humility is their most endearing quality and the greatest virtue I strive to acquire. For it is their humility, their undying quest to learn, love, laugh and grow that has made them the women they are. It has forever earned them a spot in the *Sacred Sisterhood of Wonderful Wacky Women*.

Once again, it is my honor to introduce some of them to you.

Aloha,

# They Who are More Than Friends

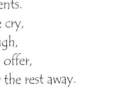

God didn't create us with the same blood line...
But He might as well have.
For you and I have mixed our diversity
Into an eternal blend of sacred sisterhood
Stronger than any natural bond.

As the finger-of-fate allowed our paths to cross,
We reached out and grabbed each other,
refusing to ever let go...
Two wacky women, clinging to each other
As if our lives depended on it.

We are sisters by choice...not by chance.

How wonderful that you get me and I get you.
We accept each other "as is"...
No apologies, no excuses, no judgments.
Whether laughing hysterically until we cry,
Or crying buckets of tears until we laugh,
You embrace all the goodness I have to offer,
And then, with a breath of kindness, blow the rest away.
It's the way sisterhood should be.

Maybe God did have a hand in bringing us together...
Two soul mates, two friends, two eternal spirits.
Forever Friends...Forever Sisters.

©Suzy Toronto

# They Who are More Than Friends

When my best friend, Candy, died of Ovarian Cancer, I felt as if a piece of my life shattered like a fragile antique mirror. Frame still intact, I found myself going through the grieving process with each shard cutting deeper the sense of loss I felt, reminding me of her absence. Unlike her family, which was flooded by the love and support of friends through their grieving process, I was on my own – an outsider. It was more difficult because of my promise to Candy that I would forever celebrate her life by embracing my own. Moving forward was difficult – but a promise is a promise. My solution was to go into denial. Sure, I realized she was gone, but I continued to talk about her in the present tense. Pushing her death out of my mind, I pretended to be normal, pretended to move on, pretended that I was OK. But I wasn't. I felt desperately alone. Even though I had a magnificent network of girl-friends to lean on, it wasn't the same. How, I thought, could I still feel so alone when surrounded by so many friends? I didn't want to replace Candy. I just wanted to get through the invisible pain, the profound loss and the intense loneliness. I remember praying to God, asking Him to come and be with me…to help me…to comfort me.

He sent Launi instead.

A friend to both of us from years before, Candy and I had hired Launi to manage our business, Perfect Solutions. We made hats with human hair bangs for cancer patients. Although friendship overlapped into our business relationship with Launi, she ran in a totally different circle of wonderful wacky women. That's why I was so totally taken off guard when, she called me one night about 11:00 pm, out of the blue.

"Wanna go to Hawaii tomorrow?" she said. Before I could stop myself with some logical reason not to go, I said "Yes." There was silence on the other end of the phone. "Really…you'll go? Don't you want details?" "Nope," I said, "just tell me what time to be at the airport."

As an airline employee, Launi was prone to go on spontaneous trips but always struggled to find someone to go with her at the drop of a hat. When I said "yes," she was as surprised by my answer as I was.

Six hours later, we were sitting in first class, headed back to my home turf…my comfort zone…my paradise…Hawaii. We talked, we laughed and we cried the whole way. Although we had never been really close over the years, we knew enough history about each other that all we had to do, as we floated in the crystal waters of Waikiki, was fill in the dirt. We both unloaded on each other. She was struggling with her own uncharted future, and I had my own storm brewing. Six days later, at the end of our trip, we were two wacky women, clinging to each other as if our lives depended on it. Looking back now, we both realize our lives *did* depend on it.

Where had this relationship come from? How could the two of us bond so closely in six days, when in all the years of knowing one another, we had never been more than casual friends? I jokingly accused her of hiding – she accused me of not looking. I think she was right.

I had been so close to Candy, especially during the last seven years as she struggled through her cancer, that I had blinders on. Between my husband, a house full of kids, my business and Candy, my life was full. Then in a single year, I had an empty nest, I moved 3000 miles away, and my best friend died. Put that on a stress meter. It's no wonder I kept the blinders on just to obscure the vision of my life exploding around me. Convinced that denial was the only way to survive, but knowing it wasn't healthy, I prayed as a last resort. (Why is it that we only get really serious about prayer when we hit rock bottom? There is a lesson to be learned here.) Since I was crying so hard, I wasn't listening...but Launi was. She listened and spontaneously picked up the phone to call me. The rest is history.

My relationship with Launi is as different from my relationship with Candy as night and day. Candy had been my friend, my mentor and my confidant. She was my biggest

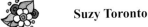 
critic and the president of my fan club all rolled into one. My relationship with Candy was one of profound growth. She pushed me to be my authentic self. She expected great things out of me and settled for nothing less. I am who I am today personally, professionally and spiritually because of her. Of this there is no doubt. I will forever love her and be grateful for the time I had her in my life. How blessed I am to have had a friend, to whom it was so hard to say goodbye.

On the other hand, Launi accepts me as is. No apologies, no excuses and no judgments. She doesn't care if I slip into a state of stupidity or rise to the top of the world. It doesn't impress her either way. She just likes me – me, with all my faults and all my fame – all my baggage and all my potential. She likes it all the same. She laughs *at* me and *with* me. She cries *with* me and *for* me. But my favorite thing about Launi is that after all the good and bad I throw in her direction, she sifts it all out, keeps only the good stuff, and then with a breath of kindness, blows the rest away.

Today, despite the fact that we both live at opposite ends of the country, Launi and I have intertwined our lives so that there is no separating us. We are grateful that our husbands tolerate our need for frequent visits and daily phone calls. They know that without each other, we'd both drown in the echoes of our own confusion. And like that day on the beach so long ago, when life threatens to tear us to shreds, we still anchor ourselves to each other and ride out the storm, lifting each other to higher ground. Through it all we have formed a bond stronger than either of us ever imagined. Far more than mere friends, we are "sisters by choice" – a most sacred kind of sisterhood – and, we thank God we have each other.

*Half of Launi's and my relationship takes place on the road. I often fly off to meet her and we take off on some half baked adventure. Whenever possible we route through Washington D.C. The connections are lousy there but we like to start out as many trips as possible by going to a funky restaurant called Sweetwater in Centerville, Virginia. They serve up these amazing Blue Crab Fritters with a lobster ginger butter sauce and roasted corn salsa that are worth the trip. They weren't keen on sharing the recipe, so you're just gonna have to route your next trip through D.C.*

*When we aren't eating groovy food like this, we settle in for some serious comfort food. These foods inevitably fall into the category of "weird-stuff-our-moms-used-to-make." Whenever someone died, got married or had a baby, Launi's Mom never missed the opportunity to send over casserole pans filled with pure comfort.*

### Launi's Mom's Funeral Potatoes
#### *...the ultimate comfort food!*

- potatoes
- bacon…about a ½ pound
- 1 pkg dry onion soup mix
- butter
- one or two cans of cream of chicken soup
- sour cream
- 1 big onion, chopped
- 2 cups cheddar cheese
- cornflakes
- salt and pepper
- milk

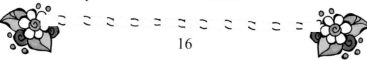

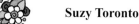
Peel, chop and boil a bunch of potatoes in salted water. Cook until done and drain. While they are boiling, chop up the bacon and fry it out until crispy. Drain it onto a paper towel. Dump out the grease, but leave enough in the pan to fry out the onions. Cook slowly until golden brown. *(The slow cooking makes them caramelized and sweet.)*

When that's done, in a separate saucepan, mix "a can or two" of cream-of-chicken soup, the dry soup mix, and just enough milk until it looks like it's "the right consistency." *(Call Launi's Mom if you need clarification on this step.)* Heat thoroughly. This isn't going to get any thicker when baked  so be careful not to get it too thin. Thicker is better. Now stir in "some" sour cream and the cheese. Salt and pepper to taste.

Toss everything together and dump it all into a "nice" casserole pan that's fitting to take to a funeral church supper.

For the topping, dump the cornflakes into a teflon frying pan and add a stick of butter. Salt and pepper quite a bit and toss them around the pan, toasting them up. Make a lot of topping as it is always everyone's favorite part. Spread over the potatoes. Bake at 350° for 30 minutes to heat through.

*Prepare to be comforted.*

# She Who Makes a Difference

She is a woman of confidence and caring...
Of loving and sharing.
Fostering a greater cause,
Her good works multiply exponentially.

She strives to make a difference...
And she does!

Ever listening to her heart to guide her actions,
She serves others with a joy unsurpassed.
Her good works seem more like fun
As she unites in an effort
To make the world a better place.

©Suzy Toronto

# She Who Makes a Difference

When she first opened the letter, Casey was a little confused. It had been almost three years since she had given blood at a blood drive sponsored by the Boys Scouts at her church. A technician casually asked if she would ever consider being a bone marrow donor. He said the chances that her rare blood type would be needed were slim, but they were trying hard to increase the pool of donors. They would start by drawing a couple of extra vials of blood from the needle that would already be in her arm. If she was ever matched, she could still decline. No big deal. All she had to do was check the box and sign her name.

When the cute but goofy boy scout had given her that paper cup filled with orange juice, the furthest thing from her mind then was what she was reading now in this unexpected letter. It said preliminary tests showed that she was a possible match for a young man who desperately needed a bone marrow transplant. She was asked to call a number to arrange for further testing to see if the match was as close as they hoped.

She stuffed the letter back in the envelope and shuffled through the rest of the mail, trying to ignore the dizzying thoughts that raced through her mind. Once again, the envelope surfaced. Once again she pulled out the letter. Then, feeling like she was almost on auto-pilot, she picked up the phone and dialed the number.

She was surprised, almost startled, that the woman who answered was not very informative or helpful. The voice on the other end quickly rattled off some canned information and blurted out a day, time and address. Before she knew it, Casey was standing in the middle of her kitchen, heart racing, with a dial tone in her ear. She decided to wait to tell her husband and children until she knew more.

The next day, Casey came to see me. "OK, so tell me." she said, "Am I crazy?"

"No, you're not crazy." I responded.

"What am I doing? What was I thinking? What do you think? I mean...well...I don't know what I mean. What should I do?"

"Breathe!" I said. "Take a deep breath, Casey. You're going to pass out. Now tell me everything."

She told me what she knew, which was actually very little. We concluded that since she really didn't know if she was a perfect match, and since getting further testing did not obligate her in anyway to consent to the procedure, she would take the next step.

"Listen to your heart, Casey." I told her. "What is it saying?"

She started to cry. "I'm scared." she said. "It's telling me to move forward."

I hugged her. "Your heart hasn't led you astray yet, Casey – never has, never will."

Two days later she went to the clinic. A very nice gentleman escorted Casey to the lab. He told her about the young man, 19, who desperately needed the transplant. He briefly explained what the actual bone marrow harvest would entail and then informed her that today they just needed to draw 16 more vials of blood for further testing. Once again, she was told that even if she were a perfect match, she could still decline the procedure.

The first-aid tape holding the fuzzy little cotton ball to the inside of her arm pulled at her skin as she drove home. Part of her was hoping she was not a match. But something was telling her differently. She was a match. She knew it.

When the phone rang three days later, she wasn't surprised to hear that the doctor wanted to see her. Would she come in and talk with him? "So I'm a match?" she asked. But the receptionist gave the canned speech that she was not allowed to discuss it on the phone and that the doctor would explain everything. That evening, after the kids were in bed, Casey walked into her husband's office and told him everything.

Mike was not happy. "Why would you put yourself at risk like this? You don't even know this person. What if something goes wrong? What about the kids...and me?"

Wrong thing to say. After 13 years of marriage, she thought Mike knew better than to act this way. Each negative thing he said made her heart race and convinced her more that she was going to go through with it.

"At least come with me to the doctor's office to talk with them and learn more," she asked. With a slow deep sigh, he agreed. He did know better than to fight her on this. What was he thinking? It's exactly the kind of thing Casey would do. That's why he loved her.

They learned more about the recipient and the procedure. The young man needed the bone marrow soon, or he would die. Once she committed, she needed to go through with it. As she looked at her husband, he smiled and squeezed her hand. He knew, at this point, there was no talking her out of it. As they walked out of the doctor's office, Mike was worried. They told her they wanted her in Seattle for the procedure two weeks from Monday. This was all happening so fast.

Casey had always joked that after childbirth, she could handle anything. But the bone-marrow harvesting procedure was not as easy as they said. She was scared, and it hurt – a lot. Almost a year later, her hip, at the harvest point where they took the marrow, was still tender even though they said it shouldn't be. But life went on. When she inquired how the young man was doing, she was told that patient confidentiality prohibited them from telling her. If both of them agreed, after a period of time, they would exchange information on their behalf. She told them *she* was willing…and life went on.

Six years later she was standing in her kitchen, going through the mail. Shuffled in between bills and junk mail was a hand-addressed envelope from Oregon. She didn't know anyone in Oregon. As she opened the letter, a handful of photos fell out, mixed with a sprinkling of glitter and confetti. It annoyingly fell to her kitchen floor.

The first photo was of a young man she didn't recognize. He was wearing a cap and gown, obviously graduating from college, honor sash around his neck – a proud mom and dad by his side. The next photo was of the same young man with a baby in his arms, a wife by his side. The photos went on: a birthday party, a wedding photo, a family vacation at Disneyland, one joyous occasion after another. The last one in the stack finally told the whole story. A very thin, very sick looking young man was smiling back at her. He was bald from chemotherapy, and his lips were covered in the tell-tale sores

**Suzy Toronto**

from the ordeal he had put his body through in order to receive the new bone marrow.

"It's him!" she cried "Mike, it's him!" Mike looked up from the kitchen table to see Casey in tears. As he jumped up and put his arm around her, she read the letter out loud, between sobs. The letter told how the young man, adopted at birth, could not find a family match to give him the bone marrow he desperately needed. He had been diagnosed with a rapidly progressive form of cancer and, after a multitude of treatments, he was told a bone marrow transplant was his only option. Since his parents or sibling were not a match, his only hope was for a donor. His rare blood type did not make his future look bright. Miraculously, a match had been found – a young mother in her mid-thirties, living less than 300 miles away. His father wept as he saw his son fading each day. His mother prayed that the donor would consent to the procedure. When word came that the transplant was a go, the young man, Jason, could hardly believe it. Someone he didn't know was willing to endure the harvesting procedure and give him a second chance at life.

Jason responded to the bone marrow without a glitch – it was a great match. Already a kid with a great attitude, he vowed to never take a day for granted. He worked hard to build his strength back up and jump into life as soon as he could. Already an honor student before his illness, Jason finished college, got married and miraculously fathered a child – something the doctors didn't know he would be able to do. He landed a great job in his field and was having the time of his life.

On his 26th birthday, Jason, his wife Debbie and 2-year-old daughter Samantha drove into Casey's driveway. As she ran out the door to greet them, Jason reached out with open arms. They both burst into tears.

Although his DNA would always be his own, his marrow was all Casey's. He was forever grateful to her for risking her life and giving him a second chance. He promised to make her proud.

It's been over ten years now, and Jason is still doing great. With two more children, he continues to make his home in the Northwest. Casey keeps a low profile about the whole ordeal. Except for a few very close friends, no one knows.

A lot of people go through life wondering if their life matters, if they made a difference in this world, if when they die, they will have left the world a better place because they lived.

Casey doesn't have that problem.

*This is the cake Casey made for Jason the day they first met on his 26th birthday. It is a cake steeped in Casey's Italian heritage and their family's favorite. Jason's wife, Debbie, has added it to their family cookbook. She makes it for him every year when they celebrate the day he was given a second chance at life.*

### Casey's Italian Cream Cake

- 1/2 cup butter, softened
- 1 tsp. baking soda
- 1/2 cup shortening
- 2 cups white sugar
- 1 cup chopped pecans
- 5 egg whites
- 5 egg yolks
- 4 cups confectioners' sugar
- 1 tsp. vanilla
- 1 1/3 cups flaked coconut
- 1 cup chopped pecans
- 1 cup buttermilk
- 1 cup butter, softened
- 8 oz. cream cheese
- 2 cups all-purpose flour

1. Preheat oven to 350°. Grease & flour three 8-inch pans.
2. Beat egg whites until stiff. In a large bowl, cream 1/2 cup butter & shortening. Add white sugar, beat until fluffy. Beat in egg yolks. Sift flour & baking soda, add alternately with buttermilk into the creamed mixture; mix well after each addition. Stir in vanilla, coconut, and 1 cup pecans. Fold into beaten egg whites. Spoon into pans.
4. Bake for 30-35 minutes. Cool in pans for 10 minutes. Remove to wire rack to cool completely.
5. Beat cream cheese, 1/2 cup butter, confectioners' sugar, & 1 teaspoon vanilla in mixing bowl. Add coconut. Frost the cooled cake. Sprinkle remaining 1/2 cup pecans on top.

# She Who Supports Her Troops

She is the very breath of freedom…
Red, white and blue through-and-through.
She understands that freedom is not cheap.
It is, and always will be, preserved by the
Blood of brave, innocent men and women.
One of them might even be her own.

There is no other way.
This wall of military might is the only thing
That separates us from tyranny and terrorism.

So she repeats the Pledge of Allegiance with gusto.
She sings the National Anthem
With a tear in her eye.
She votes to keep good leaders in office.
She writes and sends packages
To those in service.
She offers fervent, daily prayers
For their safe return.
And she is there to greet them when they return.

Indeed, she is the reason all patriots willingly fight…
For she supports her troops.

©Suzy Toronto

# She Who is a Military Wife

There is a special kind of woman
Who is so strong she can move her entire family
Halfway around the world and back again.
And even though she constantly leaves dear friends behind,
She is always able to muster the courage
To find new ones.
She has learned to be content and realizes
Wherever she is, she is home.

She understands her husband's duty
And supports him without question.
She endures many hardships alone.
She has blood that runs red, white and blue
And is always ready to defend our freedom,
Even if her sacrifice goes unnoticed.

Each time she kisses him goodbye,
She knows it might be the last time...
Nothing is left unsaid.
She assures him that all will be well,
And that forever, for always and no matter what,
She will keep the home fires burning.
She is so much more than any other woman...
She is a military wife.

©Suzy Toronto

31

# She Who is a Military Wife

Like a lot of 13-year-olds, Jimmy, my best friend's son, was a little snot. But he wasn't the only one. For four consecutive years, I was the Sunday School teacher for a group of the most obnoxious, out-of-control teens anyone had ever seen. They had blasted through a series of teachers the year before I got them. By the time I walked into the classroom, they had honed their get-rid-of-the-new-teacher skills down to a science. And Jimmy led the pack.

But, despite it all, I really liked Jimmy. What is a surprise to some, but not to me, is that Jim has turned out to be one of the finest young men our country has. Jim is a Marine.

Half way through college, he joined the Corps. He wanted to fly, and the Marines offered a program that enabled him to follow his dream. That was the second smartest thing he ever did. The first was to marry Amy.

Amy not only loved everything about Jim, she understood how important his career was to him and how he loved the Corps. She willingly embraced the difficult role as a military wife and vowed to stand by his side. With two small children

**Suzy Toronto**

and her husband constantly gone for flight training and military obligations, Amy was a real trooper.

As Jim was finishing the final days of his training, before receiving his Wings, Command briefed the men about the graduation proceedings and warned them about the now-banned post-ceremonial rituals of the past. The post-ceremony "Ritual Winging" had been a long-running, unauthorized tradition in the Corps. After the ceremony, when a marine received his wings, his buddies would slug him right on top of the pin, without the safety backings on, pushing the pins of the wings into the Marine's chest and drawing blood. This is obviously some kind of testosterone thing I don't get. But hey, I love those boys in uniform, so whatever it takes! Anyway, the ritual had been abandoned because of a direct order. Apparently it had gotten out of control. It is now considered to be a barbaric hazing and is forbidden. The men were not happy with the order. They actually liked the ritual. For them it was a rite of passage. But an order was an order, and everyone knows Marines do not disobey orders.

When the big day came, Jim's whole family was at the graduation ceremony. Jim was completely decked out in his dress blues. There's nothing like a man in uniform – especially a Marine! But if Jim was "dressed to the nines," then Amy was a solid ten. As he stood at attention on stage, his eyes gazed down at his beautiful wife and their two little ones. He couldn't have been more proud.

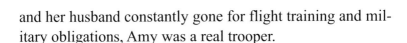

A Marine actually has his wings pinned to his uniform by the person of his choosing as part of the ceremony. This person might be his spouse, his parent or a special mentor who had had an impact on the Marine's life. It is considered a huge honor to be chosen to attach the wings, and everyone in that room knew it. Jim chose his wife for the job. When it was Jim's turn to receive his wings, Amy stood up, threw her shoulders back, and walked towards the stage. Her shiny blond hair shimmered under the lights, and her red patent-leather high heels made a clackity-clack sound. It only drew more attention to her long, sexy legs. All eyes were on her as she stood in front of Jim. She pushed the pins of the wings through the fabric of his dress blues, but didn't attach the backings. She leaned into kiss him. But instead of a kiss, she whispered in his ear, "Nobody ordered me!" With that, she stepped back, balled her delicate hand into a fist, and then with all the strength she had, slugged him in the wings, drawing blood.

The crowd went crazy. Everyone was on their feet cheering. Even the Commanding Officers, remembering their own winging ritual, broke a smile. As Amy did a crisp about-face and walked back to her seat, Jim fell in love all over again.

As wild wacky women, my friend and I always wondered what kind of girls our sons would choose to marry. Would they run as far away as possible from their crazy moms and find themselves "normal girls?" Or would they, like their

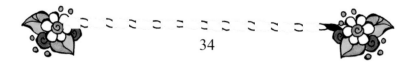

Dads, choose to share their lives with wonderful, wacky, gutsy, go-for-it kind of women?

We think Jim chose well.

*Semper Fi, Jim…*
*Thank you for your service.*
*-Suz*

### Move over "Apple Betty," this is an
# All American Apple Amy

- 10 cups all-purpose apples, peeled, cored and sliced
- 1/4 tsp. baking powder
- 1 cup all-purpose flour
- 1 cup packed brown sugar
- 1 Tbsp. all-purpose flour
- 1 tsp. ground cinnamon
- 1 cup quick-cooking oats
- 1/2 cup butter, melted
- 1/4 tsp. baking soda
- 1/2 cup water
- 1 cup white sugar

1. Place the sliced apples in a 9x13 inch pan. Mix the white sugar, 1 tablespoon flour and ground cinnamon together, and sprinkle over apples. Pour water evenly over all.
2. Combine the oats, 1 cup flour, brown sugar, baking powder, baking soda and melted butter together. Crumble evenly over the apple mixture.
3. Bake at 350° in preheated oven for about 45 minutes.

# She Who is a True Survivor

One day she woke up and her world had changed forever.
She was faced with a reality she never dreamed possible.
It was her worst nightmare, and her world was crumbling around her.

Determined not to be a victim to anyone or anything,
She decided to set a new course for her life.
She redesigned herself, her life, and her environment
To create the life she wanted for the future.

It wasn't easy.
It was an uphill climb from the start.
But the view she now has was worth
Every struggle she faced.
She has become the woman she always wanted to be.
Strong, yet tender. Wise, yet humble.
Open, loving and forgiving…
Not letting any of the past hold her down.

She never dreamed
The devastation she once faced
Would be the refiner's fire
That turned her life around.
She is now the epitome of a true survivor.

©Suzy Toronto

# She Who is a Survivor

Lemons to lemonade,
This woman is a survivor.
When opportunity knocks,
It sometimes knocks her down,
But she never lets it get her down for long.

Whether it be relationships,
Her health or professional life,
Her reservoir of love and faith
Emerges as a triumphant shining example.
She is a woman who truly knows the value of
Family, friendship, and the gift of time,
Laying aside all judgment
And giving unconditional love.

©Suzy Toronto

# She Who is a Survivor

Annie started out this life with more than a single deck of cards stacked against her. It was more like a forklift with three pallets landed on her itty-bitty baby head.

Born to a mother who was mentally ill and a father who was abusive and void of emotion, Annie grew up in a living hell. Imagine the worst nightmare a child could have, and Annie would have gladly traded it for the reality she faced on a daily basis. The first miracle of her life is that she survived.

After 16 years of physical, emotional, and verbal abuse, she finally ran away and was completely on her own. Relieved to be away from home, she existed on the mercies of anyone who would help her. Desperate for anything resembling a normal life, she went looking for love in all the wrong places. She was married at 17, pregnant by 18 and divorced by 19. Things were not easy.

On her own, again, she clung to her precious baby girl. Now, with two mouths to feed and nowhere to turn for help, she got a job and managed the best she could. Just as she was

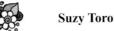 
beginning to claw her way out of the dark abyss that threatened to swallow her up, fate slapped her down again. Her ex-husband, on one of his weekend visitations, kidnapped the baby and disappeared without a trace.

The courts call it "non-custodial kidnapping," but the truth is that no one in the system much cared. She used every last cent she had, trying to locate her child. One night, as she stood in the middle of a dark, cold street wondering where to turn, she wept. She was 19-years-old, homeless, shattered, battered and alone.

But she pressed on. Despite her tragic life so far, she managed to get her GED and join the military. At least the Service would give her time to regroup. She'd have a roof over her head, a place to sleep and hopefully come out with a trade with which she could earn a living and continue her search for her child. However, before the end of basic training, a simple slip of her ankle threw her to the ground, twisting her knee and wrenching her back. She was handed discharge papers along with a small severance. And again, she was alone.

Her heart told her to press on, to keep reaching beyond her current situation. Ever continuing to search for her child, she set out to make a life for herself. She was a hard worker, and with a few good jobs, she began to shed the burdens of her past and move forward.

It wasn't easy. Change never is. The wounds of her past continued to haunt her. But each time her mind would drift back to the past, her heart would whisper, "it's over, let go." One by one, as she cleared out the closets of her life, she opened up room for new opportunities. She was able to open her heart to new healthy relationships that allowed her to grow into the person she always wanted to be. Ten years later, wiser, stronger and independent, she met the man of her dreams and married him. Along with him came wonderful in-laws – substitute parents who loved her unconditionally – the family she always wanted. There were still plenty of bumps in the road, but nothing like before. She could handle any-thing. But her commitment in the face of adversity was breathtaking.

Somehow Annie always knew that life could be what she made it. She kindled that flame and never let it die. She didn't like the one she had, so she created a new one. She reinvented herself, her family and her life. Today, some two decades later, she is happy, content and at peace with her past. Through modern technology, the help of a really great inves-tigator and a multitude of prayers, her daughter, now in her twenties, is back in her life. They are enjoying a new-found relationship as they discover the unbreakable connection that years of separation could not dissolve. As the director of a thriving marketing company, Annie is surrounded by people who love and respect her. She uses the lessons of her child-hood as a reminder of the kind of person she does *not* want to be. Instead she is kind, compassionate and charitable, reaching out to everyone she knows to inspire them to be all they can be. She is who she is because of what she endured.

As I sometimes whine about the minor set backs in my life, I am quickly brought back to reality by one very focused, roll-of-the-eyes from my dear friend Annie, who simply says, "Suz – get over it." Then, looking up from what she is doing, she raises her eyebrow and says, "If you don't like it, change it!"

It's hard to argue with her. After all, as the old lemons-to-lemonade saying goes, Annie raised the bar and took the ul-timate prize – a new life.

### Annie's Lemon Bars

- 2 sticks (8 oz.) butter
- 1/2 cup confectioners' sugar
- 2 cups sugar
- 1/4 cup lemon juice
- 1 Tbsp. finely grated lemon peel
- 2 cups flour
- 4 beaten eggs
- 4 Tbsp. flour
- sifted confectioners' sugar

Heat oven to 325°. Blend butter, 2 cups flour and 1/2 cup confectioners' sugar. Pat into ungreased 13x9x2-inch pan. Bake for 18 to 20 minutes. For filling, blend together eggs, sugar, 4 tablespoons flour, lemon juice, and lemon peel. Pour over first layer. Return to oven and bake at 325° for 20 min-utes. Loosen around edges, cut into bars and sift confection-ers' sugar over the top while warm. Soooo good!

# She May Do Foolish Things...
# But She Does Them With Enthusiasm

We all do dumb stuff once in a while.
Sometimes, in our efforts
To masquerade as a normal person,
Goofs, blunders and faux pas just slip out.

Often there is no tactful way out.
We get our feet stuck so far into our mouths
Or our skirts flung so high up over our heads
That the spectacle is hard to miss.

This is where laughing at ourselves
Becomes one of our greatest virtues.
Next time your inner "goofball" slips out,
Just throw your arms in the air,
Let out a giggle,
And give the world a cross-eyed smile.
After all, we may do foolish things,
But at least we do them with enthusiasm!

©Suzy Toronto

45

## She May Do Foolish Things...
## But She Does Them With Enthusiasm

It's hard to believe that so many mishaps, detours and faux pas could happen to one person, but Rachael takes the cake. I've known her for over 20 years, and her fun little flubbers are a constant source of amusement for me and everyone who knows her. Just thinking about her now, as I write this chapter, makes me smile. If I didn't know better, I'd think she does some of them on purpose just to get a rise out of her audience. But no, they are all bona-fide, genuine, real-life goof ups. What makes Rachael different from other people, who just can't seem to get it together, is that Rachael really is very "together." There just seems to be an invisible aura that follows her around, creating situations for a rip-roaring comedy show for anyone who happens to be blessed to be in her presence. Not only does she find herself in these situations often, but when caught, she musters up even more enthusiasm and makes the most of it.

Rachael's hilarious antics range from small, minor mishaps to all-out, unforgettable scenes that people will laugh about until their last breath. One of my favorites happened in the early nineties when she was 20-years-old. Rachael was home from college for the summer, holding down two summer jobs. In the morning she'd work at the local marina, pumping gas into boats. In the evening she was a waitress at the restaurant on the pier. This was the perfect summer job for Rachael – an avid water skier and wake border. At this point, I need to tell you that Rachael is over-the-top, cute-as-a-button. She doesn't think she's anything special, but trust me on this one, she is darling! She has a perfect body, a beautiful face and a tousle of naturally blonde hair that always falls impishly over one eye. There is no doubt in my mind that the marina owner not only hired her to pump gas, but to bring in more traffic. Boats would line up half way down the lake to have her pump their gas. All the college boys, home for the summer, would keep track of her breaks and lunch hours and be there five minutes early, offering to give her a pull behind their boats. She was loving life.

One day she was working a double shift, and she ran home after working the docks for a quick shower and change of clothes before her night shift at the restaurant. While she was upstairs blow drying her hair, she was oblivious to what was going on in the rest of the house. Two young missionaries from the family's church had called earlier and asked if they could use the house computer to type up a baptismal program. Rachael's Dad said, "sure, no problem." But he told the young men no one would be home most of the day. He instructed them to knock first and let themselves in. The young missionaries did as instructed, knocked, opened the door, announced themselves to what seemed like an empty house and sat down at the kitchen table to work on the computer.

In the meantime, Rachael finished her hair and put on the earphones to her portable CD player. Singing along at the top of her lungs to the music that was for her ears only, Rachael realized the clothes she wanted to wear were downstairs, through the kitchen and in the laundry room. As she ran down the stairs with nothing on but a skimpy lacy bra and string bikini underwear, she reached her hands up to her ears, adjusting the earphones. She closed her eyes as she wailed at the top of her lungs, doing her best imitation of Amy Grant, "Baby, baby, I'm taken with the notion…"

It wasn't until she was standing smack in the middle of the kitchen, bopping to the tunes playing in her head, that she opened her eyes. There, three-feet in front of her, were two, wide-eyed 19-year-old missionaries, complete with white shirts, dark suits and bright-red faces. As panic swept across Rachael's face, she did the only thing she could. She closed her eyes, returned her hands to her earphone and sang "Baby, baby, I'm taken with the notion,…to love you with the sweetest of devotion…" and bee-bopped into the laundry room as if nothing had happened.

Once there, she quickly got dressed in her freshly dried clothes and tried to figure out her escape. What could she possibly do? The window over the washing machine was too small to exit, and there were no other doors. Her only way out was the way she came in.

She took off her earphones, walked into the room, head held high, taking deliberate steps like a fashion model with one foot directly in front of the other and said "The *second* outfit I will be modeling today is a lively number, perfect for waiting tables at the marina or washing dishes in their back room." She then pivoted, posed and proceeded to crack up laughing. It was at this point that Rachael's mom, Tina and I returned from sitting on the dock to get something cold to drink.

"What's so funny?" I asked.

"Oh, nothing really" she said, "There was an elephant in the room, and I just introduced it to these two fine young men."

"What? I asked.

She explained what happened. We all laughed and she added, "I couldn't act like it didn't happen, so I just thought I'd own up to it." She explained that when she was faced with these frequent embarrassing situations, she had a couple of options: she could let it embarrass her to the point where she would never want to show her face again, or she could take it all in stride, embrace the situation and laugh at herself. Introducing the elephant, or acknowledging the obvious, was Rachael's way of embracing the situation and owning up to it, laughing along with everyone else.

That was almost twenty years ago. I still smile when I think about it, and I can guarantee those two young men will never forget that day.

While on my travels, I met up with Rachael for lunch the other day. Afterwards we walked along the boardwalk in Virginia Beach, talked about old friends and caught up with each others lives. As we walked along and were about to say our goodbyes, a gust of wind blew off the ocean and caught the edge of her skirt. As it blew up, she tried to tame it back down. But for all her effort, all it did was give her the look of that famous Marilyn Monroe poster standing over the air vent with her skirt up over her head. As she struggled to get it under control, three old men, all over the age of 80, sitting on a bench, smoking cigars, began to clap. Exasperated, she turned towards them, threw her arms in the air, curtseyed and said "Thanks boys."

I doubt those men will forget that day either.

Thanks, Rach, for all the smiles over the years.

*This recipe came from the restaurant on the marina where Rachael worked. She makes it for her family on a regular basis. It is my new favorite comfort food of choice.*

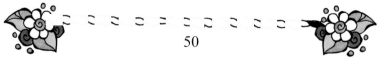

**Suzy Toronto**

## Baked Sweet Potato Sticks

- 6 sweet potatoes, peeled and cut into french-fry-like sticks
- 2-3 Tbsp. olive oil
- Kosher salt
- fresh ground black pepper
- sour cream for dipping

1. Preheat the oven to 425°.
2. In a plastic bag, combine the sweet potatoes & oil. Close the bag and shake the daylights out of it until the fries are evenly coated. Dump them out onto two large oiled baking sheets and spread the sticks out in a single layer. Liberally salt and pepper, tossing them around to get all the sides coated.
3. Bake for 15 minutes, or until crispy and brown on one side. Turn the fries over using a spatula, and cook for another 15 minutes. A lot of the timing depends on how thick you make the fries. Rachael and I cut them between ¼" and ½" inch thick. If they are closer to ¼", 10 minutes on each side will do.

*Dip them in the sour cream and experience comfort food at its best. I know, you're thinking you're gonna 'half' the recipe and only do one baking sheet. But once you start eating them, you'll wish you'd made two. You are <u>so</u> gonna love me for this recipe!*

# She Who Wears a Pink Ribbon

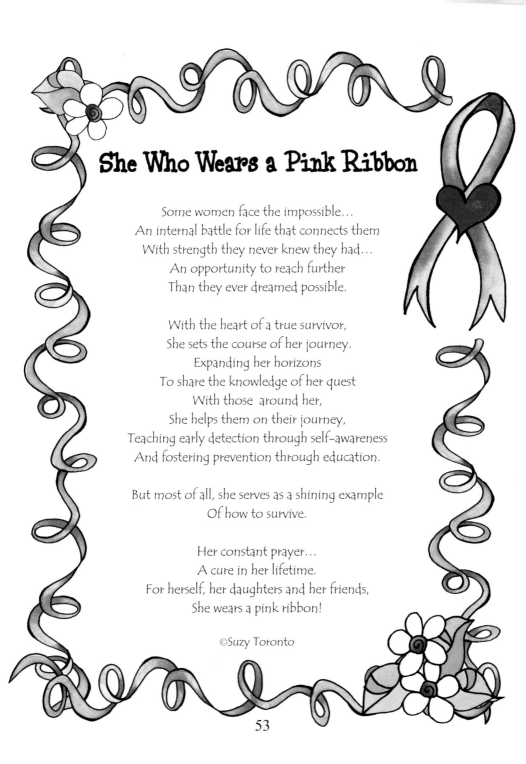

Some women face the impossible…
An internal battle for life that connects them
With strength they never knew they had…
An opportunity to reach further
Than they ever dreamed possible.

With the heart of a true survivor,
She sets the course of her journey.
Expanding her horizons
To share the knowledge of her quest
With those around her,
She helps them on their journey,
Teaching early detection through self-awareness
And fostering prevention through education.

But most of all, she serves as a shining example
Of how to survive.

Her constant prayer…
A cure in her lifetime.
For herself, her daughters and her friends,
She wears a pink ribbon!

©Suzy Toronto

# She Who Never Gives Up

Everyone faces
His or her own set of challenges.
Some are astronomical,
While others are minor.
However, at times the odds
Seem insurmountable,
And it looks like there is no way out.
This is when you need to say out loud,
"Defeat is NOT an option!"
Life is about attitude and tackling it with
The strength of a champion, not the weakness of a child.
Getting through tough times with grace,
Style and conviction is always the key.
So win-or-lose, live-or-die,
Repeat the riveting words of Winston Churchill:
"Never...never...never give up!"

©Suzy Toronto

# She Who Never Gives Up

As she sat on the front row of the church chapel, she could almost reach out and touch the casket in front of her. But she didn't. She was too numb to even move. She was 13-years old, and her world had just changed forever. Her mother was dead. As Jennifer looked at her two sisters, one older and one younger, she wondered how old they'd be when the dreadful cancer that had claimed their mother and grand-mother demanded their lives as well.

Her grandmother, a woman Jen had never known, was just 53 when she died of the disease. In 1963, breast cancer was in its early stages of research, and very little effective treatment was available to fight the hideous growth that claimed her grandmother's life. Despite a valiant fight, she died in the arms of her youngest daughter, Kathryn, who was only 21 years old.

Kathryn, Jennifer's late mother, had her own sad history. At the age of 41, she discovered a lump in her breast. A shock wave passed over her, and a downpour of memories flooded her mind. She felt like she was drowning in a sea of doom. History was repeating itself.

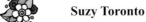 

How could this be? Kathryn had just had a mammogram two months ago. She conducted monthly self exams. She was living a healthy lifestyle. Yet still, the biopsy was positive. But with four young children, Kathryn had no intention of dying of breast cancer. Technology and medicine had made great strides since her own mother had died in her arms. She was going to fight this demon and beat it. Five years later, despite the fact that she did everything she could physically, spiritually and medically, at the age of 46, breast cancer claimed her life too.

Jennifer sat in the stiff, wooden church pew and looked around the chapel. The room was full of family and friends – all sad and somber – all staring back at her. Pity filled their eyes and Jen turned back to the front to avoid their piercing, pathetic glances. Her Dad, who was trying hard to hold it together, was busy saying something to the funeral director. Her older sister stared blankly at the casket. As Jen grabbed her little brother's hand in an effort to stifle his wiggles during the long funeral service, her little sister leaned into her and softly began to whimper. Her mind took a mental snapshot of everything around her. Unlike most of the family that wanted to just put this day behind them and get on with remembering only the good things, Jen never wanted to forget this moment. She decided right then and there that her posterity, her children, would never have to endure this scenario. This connected line of breast cancer deaths was going to stop with her.

Life went on, and the years began to give her back some sense of normalcy. Her Dad remarried, Jen headed to college, found the man of her dreams and settled into married life herself. But underneath it all she couldn't ignore the time bomb ticking away in her breast. Concern eventually gave way to obsession as her biological clock kept ticking. She spent hours on the internet searching for answers, for anything that might guarantee that she'd be spared the same fate as her mother. She was determined to not have her children face their mother's funeral before they grew out of puberty.

Information in hand, Jen began the exhausting process of sifting through the files, reports, medical articles and journals. Genetic test results and medical reports confirmed that time was, indeed, running out. It was time to act. But the conflicting pages of both testimonials and criticism began to confuse her. The process itself was making her crazy.

Trying to block out the barage of unsolicited advice from friends and family, she closed her eyes. As she did, she felt her own hands slowly reach up and caress each of her breasts. How could it be that these vehicles of such joy to her sexuality, such nourishment and life to her children were now poised and ready to sign her death certificate. She did the only thing she could do – she said a silent prayer. She sat there for quite a while. Then, suddenly, a voice rang clear and true to her heart. She knew what she wanted to do. She was going to have a preventative bilateral mastectomy. This meant surgically removing both breasts and then reconstruct-

ing them using her own body fat and tissue. Although nothing is an absolute guarantee, this procedure offered the best odds of any. This was a pair of dice she was willing to roll.

Now if this decision wasn't tough enough, an even tougher one lay ahead of her. She needed to figure out how to tell her husband and family. She could almost hear their response, and she didn't want to deal with it. She thought her husband might be turned off by the idea, and her sisters might think she was mutilating herself unnecessarily. And she didn't know how to begin to explain to her children what she was about to do. But to her surprise, one-by-one, as she explained all she had learned, they were supportive.

Six months later a date was set. The clinic she had chosen was in New Orleans and specialized in this precise procedure. The surgery was a two-part process. Using fat from both her tummy and back hip/buttock area, new breasts were reconstructed. It was not easy. During the healing process there were days when she began to doubt her decision and wonder if all the pain she was going through was worth it. But each time, she'd close her eyes and listen to the whisperings of her heart. Each time, she heard the promptings, reminding her to stay the course. She knew she had made the right decision. Through the process, Jen nurtured herself, allowing time to heal, to adjust and to accept the new transformation. She kept a detailed journal, documenting the whole ordeal both for herself and for her sisters, in case they might want to explore the same choice she made.

A year later, completely healed, Jennifer has used her experience to learn and grow and become a more empowered woman. She is now writing a book to help other women faced with life-altering decisions like she made. Although Jen is the first to admit that her choice is not the right one for everyone, it was right for her. Even though Jennifer was able to break the cycle in her generation and didn't have to face breast cancer herself, she still wears a pink ribbon. As she encourages others to be proactive with their own health, she says. "For my mother, my daughters, my sisters and my friends…and yes, even for myself, I still wear a pink ribbon."

Today, because of the marvel of medicine, Jennifer is healthy and whole with a husband who is looking forward to growing old with his wife. And because of the decision she made, Jen is now facing something her mother and grandmother never got to experience…grandchildren.

*During her surgeries, I was honored that Jen asked me to be at her side - to care for her, to stand by her and to be her friend. I flew to New Orleans and spent two weeks with her. I was reminded that, while sick, we all seem to have our own unique choices in comfort foods. Jen was no exception. This was all she asked for...over and over again. I must have made at least three batches of this stuff, and she just tanked it down. Weird what comfort foods we gravitate to when we are sick.*

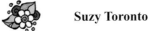 **Suzy Toronto**

*This recipe is great to eat as a salsa with chips, on top of a tostada or simply scoop out a big serving and eat it as a marinated salad.*

### Black Bean Cilantro Salsa Salad

- 2 cans black beans, rinsed and drained
- 2 cans corn, juice and all
- 1 medium size onion diced
- 1 green pepper diced
- 2-3 diced tomatoes
- 1-2 cloves fresh garlic diced
- 1 can diced green chilies
- one bunch of cilantro chopped
- 1 16 oz. container of fresh, medium salsa from the produce department.
- 3 Tbsp. lime juice
- 2 avocados, cut into chunks
- salt and pepper to taste

Mix it all up in a bowl, gently folding in the avocado last. Let set about an hour before eating. Keep it away from Jenny or my Mom - they'll eat it all up and there won't be any left for you!

# She Who Loves to Travel

She wants to do it all,
See it all, and taste it all.
There are so many wonders in the world
And by golly,
She wants an insider's look  at each one.
She wants French bread in France,
Chicken Kiev in Russia,
Tacos in Mexico,
And hot dogs at Dodgers Stadium.
But that's not all.
She wants to hike the Redwood Forest,
Ski the Swiss Alps,
Watch the changing of the guards
At Buckingham Palace
And dive the Great Barrier Reef.

Her passport is always current…
She has enough Frequent Flyer miles
To travel around the world …
And the best time of her life
Is when she's packed and ready to go.

©Suzy Toronto

63

# She Who Loves to Travel

As a college student, I remember dreaming about my future. I wanted to get rich, retire early (say 50-ish), and spend the rest of my life traveling with my husband. Oh, those idealistic college days! Well I'm 50-ish, *not* rich and *not* retired, but I do travel a lot – almost exclusively for work. It's not the glamorous kind of travel I dreamed about either. It's like millions of other business people who wake up in a hotel room and seriously have to look at their day-timer to see what city they're in. I used to doubt business people when they talked like that, but no more.

However, I still manage to get some time for fun traveling. Interestingly, those trips are rarely with my husband. Because Al and I work and travel together so much with our business, when we do catch a week or two for vacation, we have very different ideas of what we want to do. Al wants to ride his motorcycle. Now I can be a good sport at just about anything, and I do in fact have my own little Vespa scooter. But I am *not*, let me repeat, NOT a biker babe! I know there are a lot of girls who really dig it. I'm just not one of them. So I won't go with him. (Al is so glad.) Instead, I go off on my own with Launi. I've traveled with lots of friends over the years – large groups, small groups, tours, you name it. But nothing beats a trip with Launi. No matter where we go we have a great time.

Launi is a retired airline employee. She travels on her Lifetime Flight Benefits, and I tag along either on a buddy pass or use up the kajillions of frequent flyer miles I've accumulated over the years. Our trips start something like this.

My phone rings at 2:30AM. "Wanna go someplace?"

"OK," I say, "Where?"

"I don't know, I'm in Atlanta," she says, "How soon can you get here?"

The adventure begins.

I get up and quickly pack. Three hours later, I board the early flight to Atlanta.

It's 7:30am, and I'm standing in front of the big electronic board in Atlanta with flight departures clicking off gates and times when Launi walks up, computer laptop open and tapped into the internet. She says, "OK, so, we can get first class to Hawaii or France. You choose."

"Since I always choose Hawaii, I guess I'll be adventurous and choose France," I say, as I yawn.

She rolls her eyes at me, "And we're not adventurous enough flying out halfway around the world on a couple of hours notice?"

We grab our little carry-on bags and run to the gate. In route Launi sees a poster for Athens, Greece. "Lets go there instead." she says.

We shift gears and head for a new gate – Plan B.

As we sit and wait for our flights to board, Launi starts speaking Italian to the man sitting next to her. After a few minutes she turns to me and says, "We have a place to stay in Greece, a villa on an island off the coast."

I've learned not to ask questions. I just nod in the affirmative.

Ten minutes go by and Launi checks flights again. There's been another change in plans. First class is full. Now we're headed to Prague. We walk to the new gate and get there just in time to board our flight to JFK for our connection – Plan C.

At this point, I need to explain our theory on traveling. Launi and I have four hard and fast rules for traveling together. Please take note, because if we ever decide to invite you to come along, you're going to have to sign an agreement that you'll abide by them:

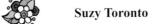 **Suzy Toronto**

Rule #1.   Pack light in a carry-on suitcase. We don't like to haul around a lot of stuff, and since we don't care if we wear the same thing everyday, we pack very light.  Since Launi and I are the same size, our wardrobe is automatically doubled when we're together. So if you want to come with us, you need to gain or lose weight to be a size 14.

Rule #2.   The adventure begins as we drive out of the driveway. If you can't deal with it, stay home and we'll send you a postcard. Life changes, and so do our trips.

Rule #3.   We only fly first class, if we're flying for free. If we are paying for a ticket, we buy the cheapest one that can get us from Point A to Point B. But if we are flying for free, we get picky. I know this sounds turned around, but it is a rule we pretty much have chiseled in stone. This is especially true on a transatlantic flight. We like to be pampered and stretch out in those big, comfy seats. And it is especially satisfying when they're free.

Rule #4.   When we get where we're going, we do "nothing." No sight seeing, no searching out ancient ruins, no visits to historic landmarks. We settle into the spot we find ourselves in and proceed to do some very serious "nothing." We have mastered this art, and we do it second-to-none. Launi and I are the only people I know who will travel half way around the world, sleep until noon everyday and then take a nap to recover.

Anyway, long story short – or should I say long trip short – seventy-two hours later, I open one eye and peer into the sun, palm fronds gracefully making a pattern of shadows across my legs. The surf is pounding against the shore, and we've been sitting on the same chaise lounges for three days straight. When a stud-muffin, cabana-boy brings us guacamole and Diet Cokes, I tip him well, so he will keep bringing more. As I hear a Mariachi band playing in the distance, I turn to Launi and say, "I forget, what town are we in?"

"Plan E…Suzy…we're in Cancun."

I think this through for a minute, trying to absorb my surrounding and say "Wanna go do something?"

Without missing a beat she says "Nope."

I smile. "Me either."

As I start to doze-off under the Mexican sun, I realize that there's no one I'd rather travel with than Launi. How blessed I am to have a friend who I can do nothing with, and in the end, feel so fulfilled doing it. This was my dream all along.

*I used to think that plain ol' naked avocados, with nothing but a pinch of salt, was the best way to make guacamole. That was until I tasted this recipe from one of the chefs at our favorite hotel in Cancun, the Westin. The chef, who was the wife of our cabana boy, quickly became our new friend, and shared her personal recipe with us. We hold this recipe responsible for at least a ten-pound weight gain that trip. Together, Launi and I ate way more than our share.*

### Guacamole

- 2 avocados - halved, peeled, and pitted
- 1/2 lime, juiced
- 1 fresh jalapeno pepper, seeded and minced
- 1/2 cup chopped cilantro
- 1/2 cup diced tomatoes
- 1/4 cup minced onion
- 1 1/2 tsp. minced garlic
- 1/4 tsp. salt to taste

*For an added treat, make up these burgers and top it with the Guacamole. You'll think you died and went to heaven. Seriously, these are sooo totally worth making!*

### Maria's Hamburgesas Maravillosas

- 2 pounds lean ground beef
- 1/2 lime, juiced
- 1 tsp. chili powder
- 1/2 cup chopped cilantro
- 1 tsp. minced garlic
- 1/2 cup diced onion
- 6 slices Monterey Jack cheese
- 6 hamburger buns buttered and grilled

Mix up the first 6 ingredients. Grill 'em, top 'em with cheese and slap 'em onto those grilled buns. Lather on a big scoop of guacamole and eat! – Yum

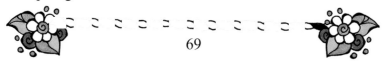

# She Who Loves to Shop

She loves a good deal,
And the hunt is the best part.
None of this "buy it, bag it, take it home"
Stuff for her.

She doesn't just want a $10 pair of shoes.
She wants a pair of designer shoes,
Regularly sold for $360.
Only she wants them marked down to $180.
Then with another 50% off
The lowest price marked
And with her "Valued-Customer" discount
She's down to $30.

Of course there is that $5 off coupon
She's been carrying around for weeks
And the store credit
Tucked in the back of her wallet…
Why, she walks off with the shoes
For only $10!
She just loves to shop!!!

©Suzy Toronto

71

# She Who Loves to Shop

For those of you who know my family, I could save us both a lot of time by writing this entire chapter with a single word: "Coke." I wouldn't have to say or explain another thing.

No, I'm not talking about the fizzy, cola soft drink or the powdery white drug. I'm referring to my Mama, the original Wild Wacky *Wonderful* Woman. Her birth certificate reads Colleen. But from the day she was born, everyone just called her "Coke." (Don't forget the quotation marks around her name – it makes her nuts.)

Without exception, "Coke" is "She Who Loves to Shop." Luckily, she's not one of those out-of-control shopaholics who spends her life savings hoarding tons of stuff. She's actually quite picky – very selective about what she's willing to add to her home or closet. She couldn't care less about accumulating a lot of things – rather she is into the whole shopping experience. For her, it's all about "the hunt."

Shopping with her is an event not to be missed. I never give up the chance to tag along. However, preparation for a day with "Coke" does take some training. Building up enough stamina to keep up with Mama takes some effort. Even though she is almost 80 years old, she can run circles around me. The day starts with Mama walking into the first store. In ten minutes, she has the whole place cased-out top to bottom. She can tell you in great detail if there is anything of value or just plain cute in the store. Not only that, but in that same ten minutes, she will know the names and personal life stories of three saleswomen and the medical history of at least two more. Nothing gets past her.

At this point, if Mama decides the store is worthy of a second look, the fun begins. She systematically starts to look through racks of clothes, shelves of shoes and mountains of gee-gaws, sorting and sifting to find the treasure buried deep in the bottom of the pile. Once unearthed, she ceremoniously presents the items to me and shoves me into a dressing room.

I hate this part. With my mother being a perfect size 6 and my sister having size 4 jeans bag on her, walking into a dressing room with armfuls of size 14 and 16 clothes is a cruel reminder that I did not get the skinny gene in the family. Instead, I got a love for all things chocolate. Nevertheless, with a big party, a gallery debut, or a personal appearance looming in the future, I forge ahead into the dreaded dressing room with 360 degree mirrors.

Now if you ever need an honest critic or a loyal cheer leader to support you in your journey to the dressing room, my Mama is the girl for you. Before I can even get myself shimmied into an outfit, Mama has already put the nix on it and is taking the next item off the hanger. Trusting her eye is always the right thing to do. Once in a while, I think I know better and buy something without her nod of approval. Later, when I see a photo of myself wearing the item, I am mortified that I even thought I looked cute in the contraption. Mama surely missed her calling as a personal stylist. Today I settle on a darling outfit that Mama guarantees makes me look three sizes smaller and 10 years younger. This, as Martha Stewart would say, "is a good thing." The tag says $89 – a price I am more than willing to pay for such a miracle.

Finally, with the decision made, and having previously spent a substantial amount of my retirement fund buying Spanx to hold everything in so nothing jiggles, I head to the cash register.

At this point I have several things in my favor. The only reason we are in this specific store on this particular day is that Mama has already scoped out the newspapers and seen the 25%-off-everything-storewide ad. Also, it's senior citizen day, so that's another 10% off. Now she starts to dig in her purse. Out comes the customer-appreciation coupon for 20% off and the store credit she has been carrying around for 4 months. When the sales-clerk announces the balanced owed is only $10.63, my mother stifles the grin that is ready to burst across her face. As she pays the woman, she leans over to me and says, "Happy Birthday Baby Girl." We head to the car, victorious with our treasure, "the hunt" a complete success.

As I get Mama settled into the car for the drive home, the look of contentment on her face is priceless. She has turned two hours at Stein Mart into a peak life experience and is quite proud of herself. Mission accomplished.

We head to lunch at Mama's favorite restaurant. She decides life is too short, so we skip the meal and go straight for dessert. As we dip our spoons into a shared chocolate lava cake, I think to myself how blessed I am to have this day with my mother, and wonder how many more I will have as she approaches her 80th birthday. But I quickly bring myself back to the present and take a mental snapshot of this moment. I vow never to forget it.

Now, I have always professed that "things' are not important, and that we are not the accumulation of all our stuff. I've always tried to remind myself that it's what's on the inside that matters most. However, when I am getting ready to go some place special, and I'm feeling frumpy, I know I can always put on my little $10.63 dress that Mama bought me and be assured that I look like a million bucks. And as every woman knows, that feeling is priceless.

Thanks Mama, for all the wisdom you gave me, for the life skills you taught me and for the unconditional love you continually pour out to me. But most of all, thanks for passing on the light-hearted, fun loving, joyful wacky gene – truly, my greatest asset.

*For all the talent, skills and wisdom my Mama has, cooking is not one of them. She claims she only has a kitchen because it came with the house and every time she serves my dad something to eat, she reminds him that she kisses better than she cooks. So to spare you from any of her tried and failed recipes, I have instead included one of mine, her favorite dessert that I will make for her 80th birthday. (Oh wait, I forgot. Life is short. I guess I'll just make it right now, head over to see her with two spoons, and we'll dig right in.)*

### Mama's Favorite Pineapple Angel Food Dessert

- 1 can (20 oz.) crushed pineapple in juice, do NOT drain
- 1 pkg. (3.4 oz.) vanilla instant pudding
- 1 carton (8 oz.) frozen Cool Whip, thawed
- 1 ready made round angel food cake, cut into 3 layers

1. Cut the purchased angel food cake horizontally creating three layers. *Make sure you do this first.*
2. Now stir the pineapple and dry pudding mix together. Gently stir in Cool Whip.
3. Here's the part where you need to work quickly because the mixture actually starts to set up. Spread 1/3 of the mixture between each layer of cake and the last third on the top allowing it to smoosh out the sides.

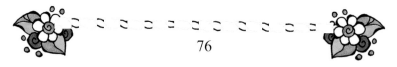

4. Refrigerate it for at least one hour and even overnight is okay if you want to make it a day ahead. Sometimes I top it with berries when they are in season.
5. Now make it for someone you love, take it over to her, sit down and dig in. Relish the moments you have with her and enjoy.

*I actually make this recipe a lot. It is so easy and everyone I ever make it for raves. I am usually a diehard real whipped cream person, but for this recipe, you do have to use a frozen whipped topping like regular ol' Cool Whip. I know the recipe sounds like one of those goofy, old fashion church-supper recipes, but this is one you're gonna have to trust me on. It's truly yummy.*

# She Who Reaches Out
# of Her Comfort Zone

Most of us spend our time neatly tucked away,
All safe-and-sound, in our tidy little lives.
It's not that we don't long for a change…
It's just that sometimes we get so busy
And caught up in the thick of thin things,
We forget how to really live.
Everything in our lives begins to take on a shade of gray.

That's when it's time to bust loose,
Abandon all fears and push ourselves
Out of our comfort zones
Into the magical, mystical, uncharted territory called
"Possibility."

Oh, sure, it is hard at first.
You may even get bumped back a few times.
But in the end, it will be worth it.
Because if you keep on reaching,
One of these days you'll make it…
And nothing will ever
Be the same again!

©Suzy Toronto

79

# She Who Reaches Out of Her Comfort Zone

As many of you know from reading my first book, at the age of 29, I married my husband Al, a widower. His first wife, Jane, died of breast cancer. She left behind four children, a loving extended family and an entire town of friends. Helplessly, hopelessly in love with Al, the kids, and with only a slight tolerance for the dog, I jumped into the marriage with both feet. Believing it was the best move for the kids to not be uprooted after the trauma they had already endured, I sold *my* home and moved into the log house, in the small mountain community, Al and Jane had called home. I really believed I could come into this charming village, give up my career, throw myself into a life of service, and be a stay-at-home-mom. I also believed that, in turn, the community and friends of the family would open their arms up and accept me. I was hoping that, through them, I could learn about Jane: Jane the wife – Jane the mother of my new children – Jane the girlfriend. I decided I'd throw myself into this new adventure and learn to call it home.

Love can be so blind.

After a year of the most difficult time of my life, overwhelmed with kids, cooking, cleaning and all the thankless tasks that fall under the heading of motherhood, I was desperately lonely. I'm a girlfriend kind of girl. I love having friends in my life and I had always been blessed to have an abundance of them. But no matter how I tried, I couldn't make friends. Determined to pull myself up by my bootstraps, I tried everything. Despite the fact that I was active in the community, church and civic activities, out of some misplaced sense of loyalty to Jane, no one wanted to be my friend. They were happy to let me work on projects, volunteer at the school and make bread for the bake sale, but no one would accept my lunch invitations, no one invited me to baby showers and no one thought to include Al and I in their social activities. I cried a lot.

I was beginning to think that all of Jane's friends were the most horrible people God ever created. In my pain, I didn't realize that almost everyone was still grieving the loss of their friend, and that I was a constant reminder that she was gone.

Everyone, except one.

Judy and Jane had been best friends when they lived in Texas. Their friendship bonded them together through some of the toughest times in their lives. Judy, a fiery redhead with a personality to match, had flown to Jane's side during the last month of her life. They were very close.

One day, about a year into my marriage, I got a phone call from Judy. At this point I had only met Judy and her husband, Tim, once. It was brief and awkward. They were both very kind to me, but it was obviously a situation far outside either of our comfort zones. As I greeted them in my kitchen – Jane's kitchen – it must have felt like a living reminder that Jane really was gone. As I held the phone in my hand, one year later, I was taken back by how weak her voice sounded.

"Suzy, I need you." was all she said.

Me? She needed me? Why would she want me when not one of Jane's friend's wanted anything to do with me? But before I could utter a sound, she turned the phone over to her husband, who filled in the details.

Judy had just had cosmetic surgery, a face lift. All had gone well until she suddenly took a turn for the worse and complications set in – the kind that only happen to one-in-a-million patients. Judy developed a blood clot and an infection. It required a trip to the emergency room. Now out of critical care, Judy was home. Emotionally, physically and mentally spent, she needed a friend – but her best friend was dead.

"Look Suzy," Tim said, "Judy's feeling pretty low. On top of all the medical issues, she's feeling guilty over having had this elective surgery to begin with. She is home now, stable and on her way to recovery. But I have a business trip to

Europe for the next eight days. I don't feel good about leaving her alone. All she's been saying is she wants Jane. Then last night she said, 'Call Suzy.' I know you don't know her well, but will you come?"

Without missing a beat, I said, "Yes."

The next morning I was boarding a flight to Austin, Texas, hoping I'd recognize Tim at the airport. But it was easy. Tim's graciousness and southern hospitality made me feel right at ease the second he threw his arms around me and gave me a big ol' Texas-size hug. Less than an hour later, when I walked into Judy's bedroom, where she laid propped up with pillows and ice packs, she started to cry. As she poured out her heart to me about her predicament, how she missed Jane and needed a friend, I started to cry too.

Over the next eight days, we laughed, we cried, and we talked endlessly about Jane. I read to her, and we joked about her swollen face. In the last few days, I helped make her presentable enough to venture out into public again. As she said goodbye to me, she thanked me profusely, proclaiming she could never have done it without me.

How had she known this was just what I needed? How was she able, in her time of need, to reach out, far beyond her comfort zone, to someone even more needy than herself? My days in Judy's service were eight of the most fulfilling days of my life. As I filled her cup and helped nurse this previous stranger back to health, my cup was filled too. Spending those eight sacred days with Judy gave me the time and distance to remember who I was and what I was capable of doing. I gained the courage to face my situation at home again. As I got off the airplane and headed back to my mountain home, I realized then and there that life was too short to be anywhere I wasn't wanted. Al and I sold our home and moved to Coeur d'Alene, Idaho. We bought a beautiful place on Hayden Lake and started over again. It was wonderful. Our kids blossomed, and so did I.

Over the next several years, Judy and I took a few girly trips together and had a lot of fun. We lavished ourselves in mud baths in Seattle, tried to experience death-by-chocolate in Victoria, BC and walked the beaches of the Oregon coast. Each time we left each other with our spirits renewed and our hearts uplifted. Through Judy, I came to love Jane. The once imaginary line that had divided us from our safe, secure comfort zones disappeared. It became a place of love, friendship, and growth.

Our lives eventually drifted in different directions. Several years ago, I tried to contact Judy and learned from her children that she had passed away. She had a very rapidly progressing form of ALS and died shortly after diagnoses. My heart is saddened when I think about her being gone.

But every once in a while I get an email from her youngest son, proudly showing off a picture of his little boy,

Judy's grandson. In the eyes of that feisty little redhead, I see the same fun, joy and compassion I remember in Judy. And it makes me smile.

Thanks Judy, for being the kind of friend that made Jane proud.

*I made this for Judy several times during the week I spent with her while she recuperated. We started by eating it with tortilla chips but after a while, we gave up on the chips, just grabbed a couple of spoons and dug in. Bonding was never so delicious!*

### Spinach Artichoke Dip

- 1 can artichoke hearts, drained, finely chopped
- 1 pkg. frozen chopped spinach, thawed, drained
- 1 cup grated parmesan cheese
- 3/4 cup mayonnaise
- 1 cup shredded mozzarella cheese
- 1/2 tsp. garlic powder

1. Mix all ingredients; spoon into pie plate.
2. Bake for 20 minutes or until heated through. (Do not use a microwave… it's just not the same!)

# She Who Loves New Shoes

I love to go barefoot.
I love to wiggle my toes in the sand.
That doesn't mean I don't like shoes.
As a matter of fact, I love new shoes.

You want to compliment me?
Don't tell me I have great hair
Or that I look
Like I've lost a few pounds.
Just tell me I have cute shoes…
That'll make my day.
I'm just apt to hike up my skirt,
Click my heels
And dance you a jig.
I just love new shoes!

©Suzy Toronto

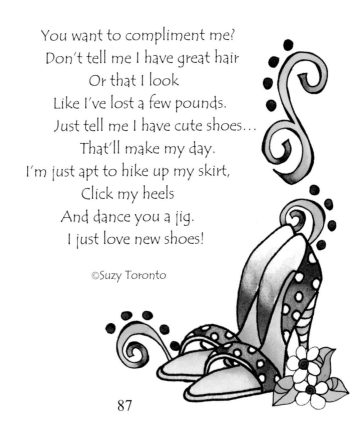

# She Who Never Has
# Too Many Shoes

I never tell him
He has too many tools, cars, or golf clubs.
So how come he constantly bugs me
About having too many shoes?
He's got to know it's a genetic predisposition,
Carved deep into my DNA…
I must have cute shoes to survive!

Actually, it's not my fault.
Those insensitive shoe manufacturers
Prey on my disability,
Making temptingly adorable shoes I simply can't resist.
I'm telling you…
It's out of my control.

Yeah, so I have a few pair…
All right, more than a few pair.
But, to my defense, half of them are flip-flops.
And everyone knows that flip flops don't count
When he says you already have too many shoes!

©Suzy Toronto

89

# She Who Loves Shoes

I love shoes.

Now you must think this is crazy, coming from a woman who is barefoot most if the time, and who has built her art around that fact. But I have to admit, I am addicted to shoes. I absolutely hoard them. My dear friend Candy, who died from ovarian cancer back in 2003, was a shoe nut too. Although she was not so much into quantity, she did have a bunch of cute ones. If the saying is true, that "She who dies with the cutest shoes, wins," I have bad news. The game's over. Candy won. I've never seen so many cute shoes as she had in her closet after the funeral. I only wish I wore her size. But my obsession with shoes doesn't come from the fact that there are just so many cute ones out there. It stems from a slightly sad story about lack of self-esteem from my childhood.

I was one of those kids who got her growth spurt in one spontaneous explosion that left me at my full height and bone structure by my 11th birthday. At five-foot-nine and 105 pounds, my large bone structure was even more exaggerated. I stood out among all my friends. I was taller than my 16 year old sister by an inch and had large size 10-1/2 wide feet to match. I was a stick with duck feet. My long, blonde, almost white hair and bright blue eyes just added to the oddity that I was growing up in Hawaii in the late 60s. Hawaii is a multicultural melting pot of mostly petite Asian and Polynesian girls with jet-black hair and dark, exotic features. I can remember coming home from school one day and begging my mom to dye my hair black so I'd fit in better. Thank goodness she didn't! Can you imagine how my platinum blond eye brows and eyelashes would have looked, framed by a head of dyed black hair? (Thanks, Mom, for saying, "No.")

But back to shoes…Fortunately shoes were optional at most places on the island. Most of the time I could only get my size 10-1/2 wide feet into a pair of men's rubber flip flops. I was always on the lookout for a non-gender-specific color and style. But there were a few situations that called for shoes – real "girl" shoes.

This is where my challenge came in. In the late 60s, on a little island in the middle of the Pacific where most petite women there never wore larger than a size 6, choices were limited. Catalogs from the mainland offered my size, but only in matronly, orthopedic varieties that looked like something worn in a soviet-block country by female shot-put champions. So instead, we'd shop the Ala Moana Mall, hoping to find something that would fit. Shopping was horrible. We'd walk into a shoe store and my mom, who has a loud booming voice second only to mine, would ask the cute little Asian shoe man if he had anything in size 10 1/2 wide. The man, along with everyone in the store, would look down at my feet as if to catch a glimpse of an oddity only reserved for those with a paid ticket to Ripley's Believe-It-or-Not. The salesman would shake his head as I tried to slither out the door before any of the Japanese tourists got their cameras out. This whole situation, experienced over and over again, did not help my self esteem. Many times I remember whining to my mom, asking her what we'd do if my feet kept growing. Instead of answering me, she'd hit me with one of her famous platitudes (she has thousands): "There was a girl who cried because she had no shoes until she met a girl who had no feet." Then she would try to boost my spirits. Usually we'd sit together at the counter at Longs Drug Store, still shoeless, and commiserate by sharing a piece of coconut cream pie.

Once however, we lucked out and found a pair of large, slip-on mules with a bow across the toe. They were a bit too small, but they were backless, allowing my heels to hang out over the edge. They hurt my little toes like crazy, but at least they didn't look like something a grandmother would wear. I was able to endure them in short spurts. I owned them as my only pair of shoes for three years. They started out as white leather, got resoled yearly and then, in an effort to suck as much life out them as possible, Mom had them dyed different colors in an effort to hide the wear. I hated those shoes after three years, yet I lived in a panic of what

I'd do if they ever got to the point where they were no longer repairable.

By the time I moved back to the mainland, it was only slightly easier to find stylish shoes in my size. But somehow I survived my shoe trama. Today, the options for a size 10-1/2 wide shoe are wider – thank you Nordstroms. But every time I find a pair of shoes that do fit, I have this compulsion to buy them, cute or not, in every color they come in. And then, after they have served their purpose and lived out their lifespan, I can't bear to get rid of any of them. I have shoes in my closet I haven't worn in years that are so worn out that they are not fit to give to Goodwill, but I almost go into an anxiety attack if I have to throw them out. So I hoard them.

Today, when I come home from the store with shoe boxes in tow, my mom, who now lives with me, is just as excited as I am to put another pair in my closet. She still remembers this silly little trauma of my childhood and each time tells me "It's okay Suzy, you just buy all the shoes you want. You're making up for lost time!" My husband, however, just shakes his head. He knows better than to say anything. I add them to my stash and remind him it's a cheap fix and shoes are simply my drug of choice.

It is interesting that all the characters of my life's work, *The Sacred Sisterhood of Wonderful Wacky Women*, are noted for their wild hair, faceless heads and bare feet. I am continually asked why they have these traits. As I finish telling them the "Why no Faces" story about my adopted son, wanting to know what his birth mother looked like and how I drew a little faceless woman so he could imagine her face himself, I quickly add that their bare feet are the result of my growing up in Hawaii and the fact that I rarely wear shoes. Well now you know the real story. The fact is, all my wacky characters have size 10-1/2 wide feet and just can't find a pair of shoes that fit.

Regardless of the stash of shoes that now fill my closet, if I ever get the chance to meet you, look down. Most likely you'll see the cutest pair of size 10-1/2 wide bare-feet you ever saw!

*This is my favorite cream pie. It originally came from our neighbor who lived down the street from us in Hawaii and owned the local bakery. As a kid, I can remember my dad out in the backyard, shucking the coconuts with a hatchet and scooping out the sweet coconut meat to use in this recipe. Today I make it with regular unsweetened coconut from the store, and it is still delicious.*

# Coconut Cream Pie

- 1 cup white sugar
- 1/2 cup all-purpose flour
- 1/4 tsp. salt
- 3 cups milk
- 4 egg yolks
- 3 Tbsp. butter
- 1 1/2 tsp. vanilla extract
- 1 cup flaked coconut
- 1 (9 inch) pie shell, baked (I love the ones by Marie Calendar in the frozen food section... but if you are a do-it-yourselfer, knock yourself out!)

1. In a medium saucepan, combine sugar, flour and salt over a medium heat; gradually stir in milk. Cook and stir over medium heat until the mixture is thick and bubbly. Reduce heat to low and cook 2 minutes more being really careful not to burn it. Remove the pan from heat.
2. Separate the egg yolks from whites. Beat the egg yolks slightly. Gradually stir 1 cup of the hot mixture into yolks. Return the egg mixture to the saucepan and bring the entire mixture to a gentle boil. Cook and stir 2 minutes before removing the pan from heat.
3. Stir butter, vanilla, and coconut into the hot mixture. Pour the hot filling into the baked pie crust. Cool. Cover and chill to store the pie if not serving immediately.
4. Top with lots of whipped cream.

# She Who Still Believes in Santa

She's tired of folks complaining
About the commercialism of Christmas
And about Santa Claus.

She loves everything about Christmas…especially Santa.
She loves the concept of Old Saint Nick …
His kindness, giving, charity and love.

For her, it's magical and enchanting
To watch the kids line up to sit on Santa's knee.
They all seem just a tad nervous to face the big guy…
Wondering if they'll make his "nice" list.

The excitement of Christmas Eve news reports
Of "Santa Sightings" make it all the more real.
(After all, if it's on the ten o'clock news, it must be true!)

Folks talk about how old they were
When they stopped believing in Santa Claus.
But it's not age that stops people from believing…
It's a state of mind.
And she's never going to get there.
She still believes!

©Suzy Toronto

97

# She Who Celebrates Christmas
# All Year Long

In February, she's still listening to Bing Cosby
Swoon "White Christmas,"
And she lullabies any baby she holds with "Silent Night."

In mid-summer, her home is the very enchantment
Of a candied gingerbread house
As the outside is illuminated
With twinkle lights despite the sultry heat.

By September, she's got the Christmas movies
In the VCR on a regular basis and is already scouting the woods
For the Perfect tree to cut down.
By November, she's totally caught up
In the dreamlike wonder of the holiday season.

In her heart is the music of Christmas calm and peace.
Her dream is a vision of Christmas magic and wonder.
Her soul is filled with the promise of Christmas Joy and Love.

She is the Spirit of Christmas.
And she celebrates it all year long.

©Suzy Toronto

# She Who is Christmas

One day I was dropping off a big bowl of potato salad at Chrissy's house for her annual 4th of July party. I swear, I could have been blindfolded, driven around the block four times until I was dizzy, drug into her house with a bag over my head, and I would have known in a heartbeat I was at Chrissy's house. The music was a dead give-away. Despite the fact that it was July 3rd , with the temperature at 91° and sunny, I heard the soothing sounds of Bing Crosby crooning "White Christmas." As I let myself in the back door and walked into her kitchen, Chrissy was sipping on lemonade, slicing fresh strawberries and singing along at the top of her lungs. As I set my large bowl down on her countertop and wiped the sweat off my brow I jokingly said, "Merry Christmas."

She smiled at me and kept on singing, even more melodramatic and acting dreamy as she started in on the second chorus "I'm dreaming of a White Christmas…"

"Any reindeer sightings yet?" I asked.

"Don't be silly." she said, "It's still another 174 days away!"

I smiled as I walked out to the car to get a second load. All of us wacky women are quite tolerant of Chrissy's obsession with Christmas. We all realize it's a genetic disorder she inherited from her mom. Chrissy, who's real name, honestly, is Christmas, was born on Christmas day. Her mom, Holly, was born on Christmas Eve, and when the two of them are together, it gets a little crazy.

Knowing this, I should not have been surprised four months later when I got a desperate call from Chrissy on her cell phone. She was at Target, talking fast and urgently as if all life on this planet depended on my obedience to her request.

"Come quickly!" she said. "Meet me in the back left corner of the store ASAP…Pleeeze!!!"

She hung up. Without questioning her, I did what any friend would do, despite the fact that it was 9:45pm, snowing like crazy and freezing cold. I grabbed my keys and headed to Target. As I got out of the car, the cold north Idaho winter air hit me like a bag of bricks. I had lived in this cold, northern climate for almost 10 years, but the tropical blood in me still had not adjusted, and I longed to see palm trees instead of so many pines. As I ran into the store, I clutched my coat around me tighter. Only for a true friend would I venture out in this weather this late at night. As I ran to the back of the store, I saw Chrissy on a ladder, hanging ornaments on a Christmas tree. She was cheerfully singing off orders to Target employees and teaching them the proper technique of hanging tinsel. As soon as she saw me, she pointed to a box and said, "Suzy, that tree is yours – do your thing!"

"What?" I said, "What are you doing?"

She climbed off the ladder and pulled me aside. "They were doing it all wrong." she said in a hushed whisper. "They were throwing things on trees and didn't care. One guy was having a hissie-fit, swearing, because the tinsel was all tangled. They were arguing amongst themselves and spoiling the whole energy."

Chrissy is big into having the right kind of energy.

"But Chrissy," I said, "You don't work here!" "I know. But they don't know that."

I looked at Chrissy. She just happened to be wearing a bright red turtleneck shirt and khaki corduroy pants – Target employee signature colors – and in fact, did look like she worked there.

Someone asked her a question, and she quickly answered as if she had the whole thing all planned out from the beginning.

**Suzy Toronto**

"You can't do this." I said. "Why not?" she replied cheerfully and went back to work.

By 2:00am, the back corner of the store had been transformed into a winter wonderland. Finished hours early because of our help, all the employees were patting each other on the back for a job well done. Through the process, Chrissy had gotten them all talking about Christmases past, memories from their childhood, and hopes for the future. No one had questioned our presence there and everyone was in a joyful mood. As we all stepped back to look at the fruits of our labor, Chrissy started to sing *Silent Night*. One by one, everyone spontaneously joined in. The energy had most definitely changed.

A week later, when I stopped by Chrissy's house, her own tree glistened and twinkled. It was not covered with the perfectly orchestrated, color-coordinated, strategically placed ornaments like the trees in Target. Instead hers was filled with cut outs of construction paper and strings of dyed macaroni, all lovingly made by her children. No presents were under the tree, and I knew there would not be many when they finally did arrive with Santa on Christmas Eve. But Christmas at her house was everything Christmas should be – family, friends and an abundance of faith. On Christmas Eve, following the caroling and hot cocoa, there would be a re-enactment of the very first Christmas. Children donning bathrobes with towels on their heads, pretending to be shepherds, would act amazed as the angel told them of good tidings of great joy.

Chrissy's youngest daughter, Noel, would play Mary and would gently rock her dolly to sleep. The night would end with everyone singing happy birthday to Jesus as they went to bed.

Yes, the energy in her home was just as it should be. Full of good tidings of great joy.

When folks talk about the commercialism of the holiday season, I am forever reminded of what Chrissy calls the "energy" of it all. It seems that most people try to cram all their holiday cheer into two jam-packed weeks of intense celebrating. They hustle and bustle around, totally forgetting the whole point of the season. But it is what we make it to be. If we throw it together because it is expected of us, if we do it to impress our neighbors, or if we teach our children that it's all about how many gifts they get, then yes, I hate the commercialism too. But if we change that energy, like Chrissy did, to truly be one of good tidings of great joy, we can bring it all it back to the true meaning of holiday – Santa Claus and all. And what a wonderful way to live, taking Christmas energy a little bit each day and spreading that warm and fuzzy feeling throughout the whole year – like Chrissy. Then any given morning we could wake up and say, "Hey, it feels like Christmas day!"

Christmas, and all it stands for, is too wonderful to get all tangled up in unimportant "tinsel." So take a deep breath, let go and enjoy. Merry Christmas.

## Chrissy's Cream Cheese Cookies

- 1 cup white sugar
- 1 cup butter, softened
- 1/2 tsp. salt
- 1 egg yolk
- 1 (3 oz.) package cream cheese, softened
- 1/2 tsp. almond extract
- 1/2 tsp. vanilla extract
- 2 1/4 cups all-purpose flour

1. In a large bowl, combine the sugar, butter, cream cheese, salt, almond and vanilla extracts, and egg yolk. Beat until smooth. Stir in flour until well blended. Chill the dough for 8 hours, or overnight.
2. Preheat oven to 375°.
3. On a lightly floured surface, roll out the dough 1/3 at a time to 1/8 inch thickness, refrigerating remaining dough until ready to use. Cut into desired shapes with lightly floured cookie cutters. Place 1 inch apart on ungreased cookie sheets.
4. Bake for 7 to 10 minutes in the preheated oven.

## Cream Cheese Frosting

- 2 (8 oz.) packages cream cheese, softened
- 1/2 cup butter, softened
- 2 cups sifted confectioners' sugar
- 1 tsp. vanilla  or almond extract

# Ok, so... This is me

Here I am, painting on my back porch - no glamour shot, no fancy hair-do or make-up. This is me, doing what I love most. When I'm not at an art show or sitting on the beach, this is where you'll find me, working on a new idea or project that kept me awake the night before.

I come by art naturally. I am the daughter of an artist, who is the daughter of an artist, who is the daughter of an artist. It's in my blood. All the education in the world cannot infuse that kind of bloodline into someone, and I feel blessed to have this legacy of women behind me. I don't remember not knowing how to draw, mold, shape or create anything. From my fine art that hangs in galleries to the variety of whimsical characters in my commercial lines, I am forever exploring new ways to express the energy inside me. I feel forever blessed to have these gifts and vow to never take them for granted.

**Suzy Toronto**

I am now 50 "something" years old and live in Tangerine, Florida in a funky house surrounded by 100-year-old oak trees. I share that space with my husband, Al, my 28-pound cat, "Bob" and a big, goofy dog named "Lucy." I eat chocolate truffles while I paint – and when they run out, I quit. I drink so much Perrier sparkling water I'm considering taking out stock in the company. I practice Yoga, which for some strange reason I think will help compensate for my horrible diet, and I go to the beach every chance I get.

I have five grown children and eleven grandkids, who love me as much as I adore them. I've taught them to dip their french fries in their chocolate shake, make up any words they want to any tune they like and to never, ever color inside the lines.

Aloha,

www.suzytoronto.com

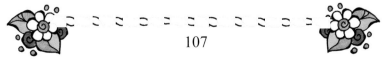